The Smallest Smudger

Written by Nancy O'Connor

Illustrated by Chantal Stewart

Flying Start
to Literacy®

Contents

Chapter 1:
A cold and frosty night

"Psst! Tomás, wake up."

Tomás's eyes flew open. It was the middle of the night, but someone was shaking him.

"It's the first really cold night of winter," said Papa. "And there will be a frost. The oranges on the trees are in danger of freezing."

"I'm going to help Papa," said Tomás's older
brother, Mario. "They don't have enough
workers to light the smudge pots in the
orange groves."

"We need your help, too, Tomás," said Papa.
"But if you want to help, you must hurry."

Tomás scrambled out of bed. Quickly he pulled on his clothes over his pyjamas and rubbed the sleep out of his eyes.

How exciting! he thought. Finally, he was getting his chance to help Papa to light the smudge pots. The smoke from the smudge pots would protect the oranges from frost and stop them from freezing.

Mario had helped Papa to light the smudge pots in the groves before, but Tomás had always been told he was too young.

Chapter 2:
Into the dark night

Tomás's teeth chattered from the bitter cold. The truck bounced over the road to the groves and then stopped. Papa, Mario and Tomás climbed out.

All around, doors slammed as fathers and sons climbed out of their cars and trucks. Everyone zipped up their jackets and pulled on their heavy gloves.

"Put on my gloves, Tomás," Papa said.
"I have another pair in the truck."

The gloves were much too large, and Tomás
could still feel the warmth of Papa's hands
in them.

Mario nudged him. "You may think this is a big adventure, but it's hard work."

Tomás grinned. "I can do it."

But Tomás was colder than he had ever been. The cold night air stung his face. His nose dripped. But he didn't complain as he followed Mario and Papa towards a big bonfire.

The workers gathered around, trying to stay warm. The men grumbled to each other, "This is bad. The cold weather has arrived too soon."

Tomás saw the frown on his father's face.
He knew Papa could lose his job if the
oranges froze on the trees. It had happened
before.

"Don't worry, Papa," said Tomás. He took his
father's hand. "Mario and I will help you,"
he said proudly.

Chapter 3:
Warm, black smoke

"Let's get started," said the foreman, as he pointed to the groves. "It's time to light the smudge pots."

Papa filled three buckets with oil and gave one to Tomás and one to Mario.

"Follow me," he said. He walked down a row of trees, shining a torch ahead of him.

Mario opened the hole in the base of the first smudge pot.

"Watch me," he said to Tomás. He poured oil from the bucket into the hole. Tomás wrinkled his nose at the smell.

Papa warned the boys to move away, then he lit the pot. With a whoosh, the oil caught fire. Thick smoke began to billow out of the smudge pot's chimney.

"It's taller than I am," Tomás said. His father and brother laughed.

They moved through the darkness to fire up the next one, then the next. When all the pots were lit, Tomás said, "Can we go home now?"

"Not yet," Papa said. "The pots have to burn all night."

They trudged back to the fuel truck. Everyone filled their buckets with more oil and started over again.

All night they moved back and forth, refilling the smoking smudge pots.

Soon Tomás's gloves were black with soot and smelled of oil. His back ached from carrying the heavy bucket. Mario had been right – it was hard work.

Tomás's eyes burned from the smoke, and he stumbled trying to keep up with Mario and Papa. He wished he was back in his warm bed.

Chapter 4:
Where's Tomás?

"Now, we are done," said Papa.

Back at the bonfire, everyone sat around with a cup of cocoa and some cookies.

"You both did a great job tonight," said Papa.   He could see Mario through the flames of the bonfire, but not Tomás.

"Where's Tomás?" asked Papa.

"I thought he was with you," said Mario.

"Tomás! Tomás!" called Papa and Mario.

Everyone ran back to the orange grove to look for Tomás.

The sun started to rise as they searched up and down the rows of trees. Tomás was nowhere to be found.

"Papa, did you look in the truck?" Mario asked suddenly.

"Ay! Why didn't I think of that?" Papa exclaimed.

When Papa and Mario opened the truck door, there was Tomás, curled up asleep on the front seat.

Papa gave him a shake, and Tomás's eyes flew open. "Where am I?"

Papa gave a happy sigh. "You had us worried."

"I'm sorry," Tomás said. "I should have told you where I was going."

"Well, both of you boys were a big help. We saved the oranges. Keep my gloves, Tomás – you've earned them."

Looking down at his dirty gloves, Tomás smiled. "It was harder work than I thought. Colder and stinkier, too!"

Papa and Mario laughed.

"The hard work is not over yet," said Papa.
"Today you must stay awake in school,
Tomás. Only then can you say you are a
real smudger, even if you are a small one."

23

A note from the author

I grew up in a town surrounded by orange groves. The orange farmers used an oil-burning heater, called a smudge pot, to stop frost on fruit trees on very cold nights. The smudge pots were placed between trees, filled with oil and lit. Heat and smoke from the smudge pots formed a blanket over the trees and protected the oranges from the cold night air.

When my brother was in high school, he worked as a smudger, helping local farmers to light the smudge pots. He complained about the hard, dirty work. He, too, had trouble staying awake in school the next day!